Horn

The Best Of The BEATLES

ISBN 978-1-4234-1050-8

HAL•LEONARD® CORPORATION

7777 W. BLUEMOUND RD. P.O. BOX 13819 MILWAUKEE, WI 53213

Visit Hal Leonard Online at
www.halleonard.com

Contents

ALL MY LOVING

Horn

Words and Music by JOHN LENNON
and PAUL McCARTNEY

Brightly

ALL YOU NEED IS LOVE

Horn

Words and Music by JOHN LENNON
and PAUL McCARTNEY

AND I LOVE HER

Horn

Words and Music by JOHN LENNON
and PAUL McCARTNEY

Gently

To Coda

D.C. al Coda

CODA

ANYTIME AT ALL

HORN

Words and Music by JOHN LENNON
and PAUL McCARTNEY

BACK IN THE U.S.S.R.

Horn

Words and Music by JOHN LENNON
and PAUL McCARTNEY

THE BALLAD OF JOHN AND YOKO

HORN

Words and Music by JOHN LENNON
and PAUL McCARTNEY

BIRTHDAY

HORN

Words and Music by JOHN LENNON
and PAUL McCARTNEY

Moderately fast Rock

BLACKBIRD

Horn

Words and Music by JOHN LENNON
and PAUL McCARTNEY

CAN'T BUY ME LOVE

Horn

Words and Music by JOHN LENNON
and PAUL McCARTNEY

COME TOGETHER

HORN

Words and Music by JOHN LENNON
and PAUL McCARTNEY

A DAY IN THE LIFE

Horn

Words and Music by JOHN LENNON
and PAUL McCARTNEY

DAY TRIPPER

Horn

Words and Music by JOHN LENNON
and PAUL McCARTNEY

DRIVE MY CAR

Horn

Words and Music by JOHN LENNON
and PAUL McCARTNEY

Moderately, with a beat

EIGHT DAYS A WEEK

Horn

Words and Music by JOHN LENNON
and PAUL McCARTNEY

ELEANOR RIGBY

Horn

Words and Music by JOHN LENNON
and PAUL McCARTNEY

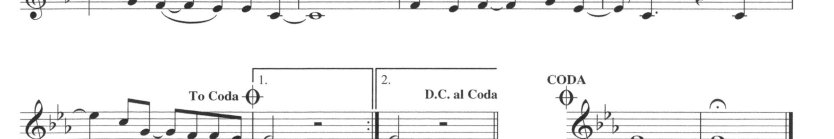

EVERY LITTLE THING

Horn

Words and Music by JOHN LENNON
and PAUL McCARTNEY

THE FOOL ON THE HILL

Horn

Words and Music by JOHN LENNON
and PAUL McCARTNEY

GET BACK

Horn

Words and Music by JOHN LENNON
and PAUL McCARTNEY

Moderately

GETTING BETTER

Horn

Words and Music by JOHN LENNON
and PAUL McCARTNEY

GIRL

Horn

Words and Music by JOHN LENNON
and PAUL McCARTNEY

GOOD DAY SUNSHINE

Horn

Words and Music by JOHN LENNON
and PAUL McCARTNEY

GOT TO GET YOU INTO MY LIFE

HORN

Words and Music by JOHN LENNON
and PAUL McCARTNEY

Very steady (not too fast)

A HARD DAY'S NIGHT

Horn

Words and Music by JOHN LENNON
and PAUL McCARTNEY

HELLO, GOODBYE

HORN

Words and Music by JOHN LENNON
and PAUL McCARTNEY

HELP!

Horn

Words and Music by JOHN LENNON
and PAUL McCARTNEY

HELTER SKELTER

HORN

Words and Music by JOHN LENNON
and PAUL McCARTNEY

HERE COMES THE SUN

Horn

Words and Music by
GEORGE HARRISON

HERE, THERE AND EVERYWHERE

Horn

Words and Music by JOHN LENNON
and PAUL McCARTNEY

HEY JUDE

HORN

Words and Music by JOHN LENNON
and PAUL McCARTNEY

Slowly

I AM THE WALRUS

Horn

Words and Music by JOHN LENNON
and PAUL McCARTNEY

I DON'T WANT TO SPOIL THE PARTY

Horn

Words and Music by JOHN LENNON
and PAUL McCARTNEY

I FEEL FINE

Horn

Words and Music by JOHN LENNON
and PAUL McCARTNEY

I SHOULD HAVE KNOWN BETTER

Horn

Words and Music by JOHN LENNON
and PAUL McCARTNEY

I WANT TO HOLD YOUR HAND

Horn

Words and Music by JOHN LENNON
and PAUL McCARTNEY

Moderato

I WILL

HORN

Words and Music by JOHN LENNON
and PAUL McCARTNEY

Moderately

I'LL CRY INSTEAD

HORN

Words and Music by JOHN LENNON
and PAUL McCARTNEY

I'LL FOLLOW THE SUN

Horn

Words and Music by JOHN LENNON
and PAUL McCARTNEY

I'M A LOSER

HORN

Words and Music by JOHN LENNON
and PAUL McCARTNEY

I'M HAPPY JUST TO DANCE WITH YOU

HORN

Words and Music by JOHN LENNON
and PAUL McCARTNEY

I'M LOOKING THROUGH YOU

Horn

Words and Music by JOHN LENNON
and PAUL McCARTNEY

I'VE JUST SEEN A FACE

Horn

Words and Music by JOHN LENNON
and PAUL McCARTNEY

IF I FELL

Horn

Words and Music by JOHN LENNON
and PAUL McCARTNEY

IN MY LIFE

Horn

Words and Music by JOHN LENNON
and PAUL McCARTNEY

IT WON'T BE LONG

Horn

Words and Music by JOHN LENNON
and PAUL McCARTNEY

IT'S ONLY LOVE

Horn

Words and Music by JOHN LENNON
and PAUL McCARTNEY

JULIA

HORN

Words and Music by JOHN LENNON
and PAUL McCARTNEY

Moderately slow and wistfully

LADY MADONNA

Horn

Words and Music by JOHN LENNON
and PAUL McCARTNEY

Brightly

LET IT BE

Horn

Words and Music by JOHN LENNON
and PAUL McCARTNEY

THE LONG AND WINDING ROAD

Horn

Words and Music by JOHN LENNON
and PAUL McCARTNEY

LOVE ME DO

Horn

Words and Music by JOHN LENNON
and PAUL McCARTNEY

LUCY IN THE SKY WITH DIAMONDS

Horn

Words and Music by JOHN LENNON
and PAUL McCARTNEY

MAGICAL MYSTERY TOUR

Horn

Words and Music by JOHN LENNON
and PAUL McCARTNEY

MARTHA MY DEAR

HORN

Words and Music by JOHN LENNON
and PAUL McCARTNEY

MICHELLE

Horn

Words and Music by JOHN LENNON
and PAUL McCARTNEY

NO REPLY

Horn

Words and Music by JOHN LENNON
and PAUL McCARTNEY

NORWEGIAN WOOD

(This Bird Has Flown)

Horn

Words and Music by JOHN LENNON
and PAUL McCARTNEY

NOWHERE MAN

Horn

Words and Music by JOHN LENNON
and PAUL McCARTNEY

Moderately bright

OB-LA-DI, OB-LA-DA

Horn

Words and Music by JOHN LENNON
and PAUL McCARTNEY

P.S. I LOVE YOU

HORN

Words and Music by JOHN LENNON
and PAUL McCARTNEY

PAPERBACK WRITER

Horn

Words and Music by JOHN LENNON
and PAUL McCARTNEY

Bright Rock

PENNY LANE

Horn

Words and Music by JOHN LENNON
and PAUL McCARTNEY

PLEASE PLEASE ME

HORN

Words and Music by JOHN LENNON
and PAUL McCARTNEY

REVOLUTION

HORN

Words and Music by JOHN LENNON
and PAUL McCARTNEY

RUN FOR YOUR LIFE

Horn

Words and Music by JOHN LENNON
and PAUL McCARTNEY

SGT. PEPPER'S LONELY HEARTS CLUB BAND

Horn

Words and Music by JOHN LENNON
and PAUL McCARTNEY

SHE CAME IN THROUGH
THE BATHROOM WINDOW

Horn

Words and Music by JOHN LENNON
and PAUL McCARTNEY

SHE'S A WOMAN

HORN

Words and Music by JOHN LENNON
and PAUL McCARTNEY

Fairly bright, with a strong back beat

SOMETHING

Horn

Words and Music by
GEORGE HARRISON

STRAWBERRY FIELDS FOREVER

Horn

Words and Music by JOHN LENNON
and PAUL McCARTNEY

Andante

TELL ME WHY

Horn

Words and Music by JOHN LENNON
and PAUL McCARTNEY

THANK YOU GIRL

HORN

Words and Music by JOHN LENNON
and PAUL McCARTNEY

THINGS WE SAID TODAY

Horn

Words and Music by JOHN LENNON
and PAUL McCARTNEY

THIS BOY
(Ringo's Theme)

HORN

Words and Music by JOHN LENNON
and PAUL McCARTNEY

TICKET TO RIDE

HORN

Words and Music by JOHN LENNON
and PAUL McCARTNEY

Moderate Rock

TWIST AND SHOUT

HORN

Words and Music by BERT RUSSELL
and PHIL MEDLEY

WE CAN WORK IT OUT

Horn

Words and Music by JOHN LENNON
and PAUL McCARTNEY

WHEN I'M SIXTY-FOUR

Horn

Words and Music by JOHN LENNON
and PAUL McCARTNEY

WHILE MY GUITAR GENTLY WEEPS

Horn

By GEORGE HARRISON

WITH A LITTLE HELP FROM MY FRIENDS

Horn

Words and Music by JOHN LENNON
and PAUL McCARTNEY

THE WORD

HORN

Words and Music by JOHN LENNON
and PAUL McCARTNEY

YELLOW SUBMARINE

HORN

Words and Music by JOHN LENNON
and PAUL McCARTNEY

YES IT IS

Horn

Words and Music by JOHN LENNON
and PAUL McCARTNEY

YESTERDAY

HORN

Words and Music by JOHN LENNON
and PAUL McCARTNEY

YOU CAN'T DO THAT

Horn

Words and Music by JOHN LENNON
and PAUL McCARTNEY

YOU NEVER GIVE ME YOUR MONEY

Horn

Words and Music by JOHN LENNON
and PAUL McCARTNEY

YOU WON'T SEE ME

HORN

Words and Music by JOHN LENNON
and PAUL McCARTNEY

YOU'RE GOING TO LOSE THAT GIRL

Horn

Words and Music by JOHN LENNON
and PAUL McCARTNEY

YOU'VE GOT TO HIDE YOUR LOVE AWAY

Horn

Words and Music by JOHN LENNON
and PAUL McCARTNEY

Moderato

YOUR MOTHER SHOULD KNOW

Horn

Words and Music by JOHN LENNON
and PAUL McCARTNEY